★ THE CIVIL WAR ★

BULL RUN TO GETTYSBURG

Early Battles of the Civil War

By Don Nardo

Content Adviser: Brent Barker, PhD,
Assistant Professor of History,
University of Wisconsin-Marathon County

Reading Adviser: Alexa L. Sandmann, EdD, Professor of Literacy,
College and Graduate School of Education, Health, and
Human Services, Kent State University

COMPASS POINT BOOKS
a capstone imprint

Compass Point Books
151 Good Counsel Drive
P.O. Box 669
Mankato, MN 56002-0669

Managing Editor: Catherine Neitge
Designer: Heidi Thompson
Media Researcher: Svetlana Zhurkin
Library Consultant: Kathleen Baxter
Production Specialist: Jane Klenk
Cartographer: XNR Productions, Inc.

Library of Congress Cataloging-in-Publication Data
Nardo, Don, 1947–
  Bull Run to Gettysburg : early battles of the Civil War / by Don Nardo.
      p. cm.—(The Civil War)
  Includes bibliographical references and index.
  ISBN 978-0-7565-4368-6 (library binding)
  ISBN 978-0-7565-4411-9 (paperback)
  1. United States—History—Civil War, 1861–1865—Campaigns—Juvenile literature.
  I. Title. II. Series.
  E470.N37 2011
  973.7'31—dc22   2010001017

Image Credits: Corbis/Royalty-free, 25, 31, 37, 54; Courtesy of Army Art Collection, U.S.
Army Center of Military History, 3 (middle), 18; Courtesy Pecos National Historical Park,
National Park Service, artist Roy Andersen, 34; DVIC/NARA, 8; Getty Images: Hulton
Archive, cover, Kean Collection, 41; Library of Congress, 3 (left and right), 5, 6, 17, 19, 24,
28, 32, 39, 45, 49, 52, 56 (all), 57; North Wind Picture Archives, 13, 50.

Visit Compass Point Books on the Internet at *www.capstonepub.com*

TABLE OF CONTENTS

4   **Unrealistic Strategies**

15   **Early Battles in the East**

27   **Bloody Strife in the West**

36   **African-American Soldiers**

46   **A Great Turning Point**

    56   **Timeline**

    58   **Glossary**

    60   **Additional Resources**

    62   **Source Notes**

    64   **Index**

CHAPTER 1
UNREALISTIC STRATEGIES

When Abraham Lincoln solemnly took the oath of office as president of the United States in March 1861, his country was torn apart. Seven southern states had recently left the Union.

The extreme move of secession hadn't come as a surprise to the new president. For at least two generations the North and South had been growing apart culturally. The South remained mainly an agricultural society that had changed little since the Revolution. In contrast, the North, while still primarily agricultural, had begun to develop small industries and a culture that encouraged growth and innovation.

The chief cause of the split, though, was the institution of slavery. Most southern plantation owners used black African slaves to do their farm work. Moreover, white southerners had been trying to expand slavery into western territories and newly formed states. Many northerners, who saw slavery as wrong, grudgingly accepted it in states where it existed but wanted to keep it from expanding into new territories in the West.

Long-festering hatred and mistrust between pro- and anti-slavery forces came to a head when Lincoln, who was anti-slavery, was elected president in November 1860. Even though Lincoln did not intend to end

Abraham Lincoln served as U.S. president from 1861 until his assassination in 1865.

slavery in the South, southerners distrusted all Republicans and feared they would lose their slaves and traditional way of life. So one by one, the southern states began to leave the Union. Between December 1860 and February 1861, seven of them seceded and formed a new country —the Confederate States of America. The states were South Carolina, Mississippi, Florida, Alabama, Georgia, Louisiana, and Texas. The Confederacy had its own constitution and chose a president, Jefferson Davis.

For a short while, the two sides—the Union and

Confederacy—managed to avoid major violence. But on April 12, 1861, Confederate forces attacked Fort Sumter, a U.S. military post in the harbor of Charleston, South Carolina. Like most northerners, President Lincoln was outraged that southerners had fired on the American flag. So on April 15 he called for 75,000 volunteers to put down what he viewed as a rebellion. Soon afterward, four more states—Virginia, Arkansas, Tennessee, and North Carolina—seceded and joined the Confederacy. An all-out civil war appeared certain.

Confederate forces shelled Fort Sumter for 34 hours.

★CONFIDENT OF A SHORT WAR

As the conflict began, people on both sides displayed a great deal of resolve and fortitude. A foreigner who visited the South in 1862 wrote: "The great strength and power of the southern army lies in the individual resolution of the men. Every private feels a determination, not only to carry his regiment through the fight, but to see his country through the war. Boys of fifteen may be seen by the side of grey-haired men."

Similarly, many soldiers on both sides were confident that the war would be short. After all, went the common wisdom, the enemy was cowardly, incompetent, or both, and therefore easy to defeat. One northerner quipped, "I hoped to see things settled 'fore this fall, the Rebbels licked [and] Jeff Davis hanged, an' all." A southern soldier boasted: "I believe that [my] brigade can whip 25,000 Yankees. I think I can whip 25 myself."

Such unrealistic views also shaped the early strategies adopted by northern and southern military leaders. At first most northern leaders assumed they would not have to defeat and capture the entire South. It would be enough, they thought, to gain one or two major victories, and then arrest Jefferson Davis and other southern leaders. Most or all of the southern states would then see the error of their ways and rejoin the Union.

Southern military leaders adopted a different sort of initial

Union Army soldiers drilled near Washington, D.C., in 1861.

strategy. It had both offensive and defensive aspects. A noted scholar of the war, Paddy Griffith, explains the defensive ones: "Numerous small contingents of troops were dispersed around [the] six thousand miles of land and water borders of the Confederacy in the hope of blocking enemy invasions at any and all points. Some of these troops were stationed in forts along the sea coasts and along rivers. Others were organized in small mobile armies."

The mobile armies were the key to the offensive part of the strategy. At opportune times, they would go on the attack and win victories. It was hoped that would cause northern armies and their leaders to lose their confidence and give up the idea of fighting the South.

Both the northern and southern strategies were naïve and unrealistic. Each assumed that the other side lacked a strong will to fight for its way of life. So neither side planned for a long, bloody conflict. Because the war did turn out to be lengthy and very costly in lives and money, the early northern strategy proved particularly unrealistic. To win such a conflict, historians point out, the South needed only to defend its territory long enough to weary the northerners. But the Union, to win, had to conquer a vast territory and crush a people. Anything less than unconditional surrender of the Confederate armies and collapse of the government would have been a southern victory.

By June 1861, 11 states had seceded from the Union.

★FIRST MODERN WAR

The two sides were also unprepared in other ways for the long, frightening, and draining conflict. First, both the North and South started with too few effective weapons. This problem was especially bad in the South. Because it was largely an agricultural society, the South lacked the industrial capacity of the North. In 1861, when the conflict started, 110,000 of America's 128,000 factories

THE SOUTH'S VITAL IRON FOUNDRY

The South had few arms factories and iron foundries. So southern armies came to greatly depend on the weapons produced by the Tredegar Iron Works, in the Confederate capital, Richmond, Virginia. Confederate officer Thomas C. DeLeon reported:

"So potent a factor in the aggressive power of the Confederacy was this foundry that it [was seen as more important than] the regular government agencies. When the war began, this was the only rolling-mill of great capacity, of which the South could boast; the only one, indeed, capable of casting heavy guns [cannons]."

The Tredegar Iron Works so greatly aided the Confederacy that the lengthening of the war may be, in large measure, attributed to its capacity.

were in the North. In addition, northern companies made almost all the gunpowder and cannons.

Another serious weakness for the South was its disorganized and inefficient way of raising troops and appointing officers. Each southern state created its own military units. Many soldiers chose their own officers, usually by electing them. But soldiers from one state sometimes did not want to follow orders from officers from another state. The Confederate secretary of war, Judah P. Benjamin, complained that "the troops being State troops officered by State officers … Confederate commanders were [often] without means of enforcing discipline and efficiency."

Both sides also found themselves fighting against or using new industrial products and technologies. They had never before been major factors in warfare. And they frequently widened the scope of fighting and made it more lethal. For these reasons, the Civil War is often called the first modern war.

For instance, it was the first conflict in world history in which railroads played an important role. America's growing railroad system carried soldiers and supplies long distances and faster than was possible before. Another new technical device, the telegraph, also played a crucial role. Northern and southern generals were the first military commanders to send and receive messages in minutes rather than days or even weeks.

★BATTLE OF THE IRONCLADS

Still another technological advance was the use during the war of the first American metal warships, called ironclads. The first, built in the South, was the *Virginia*, also known by its earlier name, the *Merrimack*. It was 270 feet (82 meters) long and covered with 800 tons (726 metric tons) of iron plates. It was powered by steam.

NEW NAVAL WEAPONS

Several new naval weapons emerged during the Civil War. Perhaps the most famous were the steam-powered ironclads—the South's *Virginia* and the North's *Monitor*. They started a trend that eventually phased out wooden warships in favor of metal ones. Another significant naval advance was the so-called ram. It consisted of an ordinary wooden steamship that had a powerful iron ram attached to its bow. Such a vessel charged at and smashed into an enemy ship. The ram opened a hole in the other boat's hull, causing it to take on water and sink. In 1862 Union engineer Charles Ellet constructed a small fleet of rams that scored a victory on the Mississippi River near Memphis, Tennessee.

The Confederate Virginia *rammed the* Cumberland, *which sank off the Virginia shore.*

On March 8, 1862, the *Virginia* attacked and sank a traditional wooden warship, the Union's *Cumberland,* off the shore of Virginia at Hampton Roads. More than 120

Union sailors and officers were killed. The southern ironclad also attacked and damaged other Union vessels.

But the next day, the *Virginia* confronted something its officers and crew had not expected. The first Union ironclad, the *Monitor,* appeared, ready for battle. Many people standing on a nearby shore watched the historic fight, which went on for hours. According to one of the *Monitor*'s officers, S.D. Greene, the enemy ship "tried to run us down with her iron prow [the ship's front], but did no damage whatever. [We attacked her] as hard as we could, the shot, shell, grape, canister, musket, and rifle-balls flying in every direction but doing no damage. Our tower was struck several times [but] it did not affect us any."

Because neither ship was able to win a definite victory, the battle turned out to be a draw. On land, meanwhile, battle followed battle, and the death toll began to mount. Two things became horribly clear to people on both sides: The war was not going to be short. And a great many soldiers were going to die.

CHAPTER 2
EARLY BATTLES IN THE EAST

In the two years following President Lincoln's call-up of 75,000 soldiers in April 1861, Union and Confederate forces fought a series of land battles. Some were skirmishes, small clashes involving few fighters. But several battles were large encounters that killed and wounded many soldiers. Many took place in the Eastern Theater, an area that encompassed Pennsylvania, Maryland, Virginia, the District of Columbia, and eastern North Carolina.

The war's first major land battle took place in the Eastern Theater. It was in many ways a direct result of a key decision made by Confederate leaders in May 1861. They moved their capital from Montgomery, Alabama, to Richmond, Virginia. Richmond was not far from the border between North and South. So many northerners called for its immediate capture, believing that would quickly end the war.

A major obstacle stood in the way of this plan, however. Confederate General P.G.T. Beauregard had gathered an army of more than 20,000 at Manassas Junction, Virginia, about 25 miles (40 kilometers) from Washington, D.C. That force would have to be eliminated before a Union army could move on Richmond.

The job of engaging Beauregard fell to Union Brigadier General Irvin McDowell. On July 21, 1861, McDowell, commanding close to 30,000 men, approached Bull Run, a creek near the village of Manassas. (Because the North and South used different naming systems, the battle became known as First Bull Run in the North and First Manassas in the South.)

★PANIC AT BULL RUN

As the fighting began, southern forces were at first disorganized and began retreating. A Confederate doctor in their ranks, J.C. Nott, later recalled: "The regiments were torn to pieces, driven back, and so overwhelmed by numbers that I feared the day was lost."

But then confusion set into the Union ranks. At the same time, Confederate reinforcements arrived. "I saw our reinforcements pouring in," Nott wrote. "No one can imagine such a grand, glorious picture as these patriots presented, rushing to the field through the masses of wounded bodies." Seeing the fresh troops entering the fray, many Union soldiers panicked. And with cries of "Drive them into the Potomac!" the southerners counter

Because of the color of their uniforms, the North and the South were referred to as the Blue and the Gray.

attacked and won the day. The Union Army retreated all the way back to the defenses of Washington, D.C.

The number of men killed at First Bull Run was small compared with the awful death tolls of later battles. By one count, 418 Union soldiers and 387 Confederates died. But the battle was extremely important for two reasons. First, it showed everyone in the North that the war was going to be neither short nor easy. (It would take the South longer to reach the same conclusion.) Second, it was a decisive Confederate

More than 4,000 soldiers from the North and South were wounded, captured, or missing at Bull Run.

victory. And that dangerously lowered northern morale while raising the confidence of southerners. "It set the tone for everything that was to follow," historian Paddy Griffith points out. "Having lost the first major contest the Federals [Union soldiers] formed a low opinion of themselves and had a correspondingly high opinion of the Confederates, [and] the Confederates came to precisely the same conclusion."

★THE PENINSULA CAMPAIGN

The loss at Bull Run so embarrassed the North that Lincoln felt he had to replace McDowell. The president put Major General George B. McClellan in command of the main Union army in the East, which was called the Army of the Potomac. But McClellan fared little better than McDowell had. Early in 1862 McClellan embarked on the Peninsula Campaign. He planned to move his army by water to a position near Richmond, defeat Confederate

President Lincoln discussed battle strategy with General George B. McClellan (right) in 1862.

forces there, and then capture the Confederate capital. He sent most of his troops by boat to the Peninsula, the area between the York and James rivers in Virginia. The Union forces moved up the Peninsula, and within two months they were just six miles (9.6 km) from Richmond.

A VERY DETERMINED SOLDIER

During one of the battles of the Peninsula Campaign, fought at Gaines' Mill, Virginia, in late June 1862, a Union soldier put on an unusual show of determination. Soldier Oliver Norton recalled:

"I returned to the fight, and our boys were dropping on all sides of me. I was blazing away at the rascals … when a ball [bullet] struck my gun … and cut it in two. The ball flew in pieces and part went by my head to the right and three pieces struck just below my left collar bone. … I pulled them out and snatched a gun from Ames in Company H as he fell dead. Before I had fired this at all a ball clipped off a piece of the stock, and an instant after, another struck the seam of my canteen and entered my left groin. I pulled it out and, more maddened than ever, I rushed in again. A few minutes after, another ball took six inches off the muzzle of this gun. [After I had picked up a another gun], a buckshot struck me in the left eyebrow, making the third slight scratch I received in the action."

But the southern commanders and soldiers in the area were highly determined and fought bravely. McClellan suffered heavy losses in a series of battles fought between late May and early July 1862, and the Union Army began to fall back. McClellan did gain the advantage in one of the engagements, fought at Malvern Hill, near the James River in Virginia on July 1. A Union artillery division, with more than 250 cannons, occupied the hill's summit. Wave after wave of Confederate infantrymen charged up the slope. They were badly mauled by the cannons, and more than 5,000 southerners were killed or wounded. But despite the bloodbath, Confederate forces managed to outmaneuver McClellan in the region, and he continued his retreat.

Among the southern generals who distinguished themselves in the Peninsula Campaign was Robert E. Lee. He took charge of the Army of Northern Virginia and quickly earned a reputation for aggressiveness and military know-how. He kept that reputation for the rest of the war. According to a fellow officer, Lee was "calm, dignified, and commanding in his bearing, [with] a countenance [expression] strikingly benevolent [and] a clear, honest eye that could look friend or enemy in the face."

Lee was not only skilled and bold, but also realistic. He felt that the fighting should be left to soldiers, and that politicians should not interfere. He daringly demonstrated this belief during the Peninsula Campaign. When Confederate President Jefferson Davis suddenly appeared on the battlefield, Lee curtly made it clear that his boss did not belong there. The flustered Davis awkwardly rode off the field.

LEE REBUFFS THE PRESIDENT

In a celebrated incident during the Peninsula Campaign, Confederate President Jefferson Davis, who had military experience, rode onto the battlefield. General Robert E. Lee abruptly forced him to leave, as recalled by a southern writer:

"General Lee observed the president's approach, and was evidently annoyed at what he considered a foolhardy expedition of needless exposure of the head of the government. ... [Lee] exchanged with the president a salute, with the most rigid reserve of anything like welcome or cordiality. ... The general, looking not at him but at the assemblage at large, asked in a tone of irritation, 'Who are all [these] people, and what are they doing here?' No one moved or spoke, but all eyes were upon the president. ... Such a rebuff was a stunner to Mr. Davis, who ... turned his horse's head [and retired from the field]."

★ "RECKLESS DISREGARD OF LIFE"

After the Union's failure to take Richmond, Lee went on the offensive. His thrust northward toward Washington, D.C., met with success in a large battle fought from August 28 to 30, 1862. Because it took place near Manassas, the site of the war's first battle, it became known as Second Manassas, or Second Bull Run. Lee's forces, commanded by two talented generals, James Longstreet and Thomas "Stonewall" Jackson, defeated a Union army led by Major General John Pope.

After this major victory, Lee and his officers were confident they could cross into northern territory and score a victory there. Such a win would surely demoralize the North, they reasoned. Also, it might persuade Britain or France to back the South in the war.

With such goals in mind, Lee led 45,000 soldiers across the Potomac River into Maryland. There, on September 17, 1862, one of the bloodiest battles of the war occurred at Antietam Creek, near the Maryland town of Sharpsburg. Some of the most savage fighting took place in a cornfield, where the opposing forces repeatedly attacked and counterattacked.

A Union officer, Major Rufus Dawes, remembered: "As we appeared at the edge of the corn, a long line of men in butternut and gray [the colors of Confederate uniforms] rose up from the ground. Simultaneously, the hostile battle lines opened a tremendous fire upon each other. Men [were] knocked out of the ranks by

*The charge of the Union Iron Brigade near Dunker
Church during the Battle of Antietam*

[the] dozens. But we jumped over the fence and pushed
on, loading, firing, and shouting as we advanced. [There
was] a reckless disregard of life, of everything but victory."

That victory ultimately went to the North. Lee lost so
many men that he had no choice but to retreat back over
the Potomac into Virginia. However, both sides suffered
horribly in the fighting. Indeed, more Americans were
killed that day than on any other day in U.S. military
history, before or since—3,654 in all, along with 17,292
wounded and 1,771 missing.

Even more men would have died at Antietam if it had not been for a nurse, Clara Barton. With bullets flying around her, she aided the wounded in a small farmhouse in the middle of the battlefield. Impressed by her courage and devotion, a Union doctor called her "the true hero of the age, the angel of the battlefield."

After the Civil War, Clara Barton founded the American Red Cross.

★ HORRENDOUS DEFEAT

With Lee out of northern territory, Union generals tried once again to move on Richmond. First General Ambrose Burnside divided an army into three sections and marched them to the Rappahannock River, in northeastern Virginia. His goal was to capture nearby Fredericksburg, leaving Richmond wide open for the taking. But Burnside waited three weeks before crossing the river, which gave Lee enough time to move his forces to the scene and take positions on the heights behind the town. Burnside unwisely ordered a frontal attack, and many of his men were cut down by cannon and musket fire. More than 12,000 Union soldiers were killed or wounded in the December battle.

Still another northern loss occurred in early May 1863 at Chancellorsville, not far west of Fredericksburg. General Joseph Hooker, who had replaced Burnside, vowed to get by the Fredericksburg region and take Richmond. Ruling out a direct attack on the front of Lee's forces, Hooker tried to go around the enemy. He ordered most of his men up the river, crossed it, then moved on Lee's position between Fredericksburg and Chancellorsville. But Lee brilliantly sent his own men to outflank Hooker. As a result, the Union forces were soundly defeated. The South also suffered a devastating loss. General Thomas "Stonewall" Jackson, one of the Confederacy's most skillful commanders, was badly wounded by his own men and later died.

Union forces lost 17,000 killed or wounded at Chancellorsville. When news of the disaster reached President Lincoln, he said: "My God! My God! What will the country say! What will the country say!"

For the moment, as it turned out, the opinions of Lincoln's countrymen were mixed. In spite of the recent losses in the East, the Union had begun to rack up victories in the West. Clearly it was much too early in the conflict to say which side had the best chance of winning.

CHAPTER 3
BLOODY STRIFE IN THE WEST

Much of the most decisive fighting during the Civil War's first two years happened in the Western Theater. The area stretched west from the Appalachian Mountains to the Mississippi Valley.

The Confederates had enjoyed several early successes in the East, but they were far less successful in the West. There Union forces concentrated on gaining control of key rivers, particularly the Mississippi. Capturing that waterway and the major cities on its banks would cut off important southern supply lines, split the Confederacy in half, and hasten its end.

★ UNION VICTORIES

One of the first key western cities taken by the Union was Nashville, the capital of Tennessee. Northern commander Don Carlos Buell forced the city to surrender in late February 1862. This was a blow to the South. The

Nashville Armory was one of the few Confederate factories capable of making cannons. Nashville was also a railroad hub that had given southern states access to many kinds of goods.

Soon afterward, on March 7 and 8, an important battle took place at Pea Ridge, in northwest Arkansas. The Confederate forces, led by General Earl Van Dorn, outnumbered those of the Union, under General Samuel R. Curtis, almost two to one. So Van Dorn thought it safe to divide his army and attack the enemy from both front and rear. This proved a mistake. The Confederate right wing had heavy

The victory at Pea Ridge helped secure Union control of Arkansas and Missouri.

losses, and Van Dorn had to retreat. The victory gave the Union control of much of the region, including nearby Missouri.

The defeated southern soldiers suffered terribly as they tried to live off the land while on the run. One of them, William Watson, later recalled:

"We had now the march before us, and we must undertake it, without provisions, without tents or cooking utensils, without blankets or overcoats, and our thin clothing now worn and ragged. ... We proceeded to scramble along the best way we could, wading through creeks and rivers and scrambling over rocks and through brushwood. ... We sometimes found the remains of some turnips or onions, which were eagerly dug out of the ground [and] eaten raw."

The North had other important objectives in the region. One was taking Memphis, Tennessee. A second goal was the seizure of Vicksburg, Mississippi. Another was the capture of the Memphis and Charleston Railroad, a key supply line between the Mississippi Valley and the Confederate capital of Richmond. If all of these goals could be achieved, the Union would gain almost complete control of the upper Mississippi.

In early April 1862, a Union army commanded by Major General Ulysses S. Grant set out to capture the railroad. Grant first took two Confederate forts on the Tennessee River, Fort Henry and Fort Donelson. This broke the large Confederate defensive line in the region.

Grant then moved his men toward an important railroad junction at Corinth, Mississippi. But on April 6, Grant's forces were hit by a surprise attack at Shiloh, in southwestern Tennessee. The Confederates were led by generals P.G.T. Beauregard and Albert S. Johnston. They tried to push Grant and his men into the Tennessee River. In the evening, however, Union reinforcements arrived. The next day Grant counterattacked and scored a victory. Still, the death toll of his men, 1,754, was only slightly higher than the Confederate deaths of 1,728 men.

THROUGH THE WOODS THEY CAME

One of the bloodiest episodes in the Battle of Shiloh, in April 1862, took place in an area that became known as the Hornet's Nest. A Union soldier who fought there later recalled how it started:

"Suddenly, obliquely to our right, there was a long, wavy flash of bright light, then another, and another! It was the sunlight shining on gun barrels and bayonets, and there they [the Confederate soldiers] were at last! A long brown line, with muskets … in excellent order, right through the woods they came. We began firing at once. From one end of the regiment to the other leaped a sheet of red flame."

★NEW ORLEANS FALLS

Less than three weeks after the bloody encounter at Shiloh, another major Confederate stronghold in the West—New Orleans—fell to Union forces. A few months before that, President Lincoln had told veteran naval officer David G. Farragut to "proceed up the Mississippi River and reduce the defenses which guard the approaches to New Orleans, when you will appear off that city and take possession of it." Capturing this city was a high Union priority. Control of it would not only deny several southern states badly needed supplies, but it would also keep the

Admiral David G. Farragut

South from exporting its most lucrative crop, cotton, from this important port.

Farragut collected a fleet of 37 warships and gunboats and moved them along the Gulf Coast and up the Mississippi. After bombarding Confederate forts along the way, the Union fleet approached the main target—New Orleans.

The entire Confederate fleet in New Orleans, Louisiana, was lost during the battle.

Northern officer George H. Perkins served on the gunboat *Cayuga*. He later described one of the furious cannon battles with Confederate batteries on the shore south of the city:

"Our ship had received forty-two shots in masts and hull, and six of our men had been wounded; one of the boys had to have one of his legs cut off. [The] bombardment [by enemy cannons] was continuous and perfectly awful. ... The river and shore were one blaze, and the sounds and explosions were terrific. ... There were a lot of treacherous rascals concealed in these [Confederate] batteries, and when we had come close enough ... they opened a heavy fire. [Eventually the fleet silenced them.] After this there were no more obstacles between us and the city."

After Farragut received the city's surrender, he was not surprised to find much bitterness and anger among the defeated residents. An example of how they felt is in the journal of an enraged Louisiana woman, Julia LeGrand:

"The blood boiled in my veins—I felt no fear—only anger. ... This is a most cowardly struggle. These people [the Yankees] can do nothing without gunboats. ... These passive instruments do their fighting for them. It is at best a dastardly way to fight."

After securing New Orleans, northern forces managed to seize Memphis, Tennessee, in June 1862. That left one last major Union goal along the Mississippi —the capture of Vicksburg. A large campaign to do that began in December.

★STRUGGLE FOR THE FAR WEST

The Mississippi Valley was not the only western region that Lincoln and his generals sought to control. Hundreds of miles to the west, the Union and Confederacy also clashed in Arizona and New Mexico, which were then territories. People in southern New Mexico Territory sympathized with the Confederacy. Early in 1861 they had broken away from the Union and formed the Confederate Territory of Arizona. Most of the rest of New Mexico remained loyal to the United States.

The region became hotly contested by the two sides in the war. Confederate troops from Texas invaded New Mexico Territory early in 1862. And a small but important battle took place on March 28 at Glorieta Pass, in the northern part of the territory. There a force of 1,300 Union soldiers met a slightly smaller number of Confederates. Though the forces were small, the fighting was intense, as remembered by the Confederate commander, W.R. Scurry:

"Three [Union] batteries of eight guns opened a furious fire of [shells and other projectiles] upon our advancing troops. Our brave soldiers, heedless of the storm, pressed on, determined, if possible, to take their battery. A heavy body of infantry, twice our number, interposed to save

The Battle of Glorieta Pass ended the Confederates' dreams of overtaking the West.

W.R. Scurry, who led the southern forces in the fight at Glorieta Pass in March 1862, penned this description of the last moments of the battle:

"Inch by inch was the ground disputed, until the artillery of the enemy had time to escape with a number of their wagons. The infantry also broke ranks and fled from the field. So [hasty] was their flight, that they cut loose their teams and set fire to two of their wagons. The pursuit was kept up until forced to halt from the extreme exhaustion of the men, who had been engaged for six hours in the hardest contested fight it had ever been my lot to witness."

their guns. Here the conflict was terrible."

The Confederates held their ground that day. But they were soon forced to retreat to Texas. The South was unable to establish a foothold in the Far West. And the North steadily gained control of the area. As the war headed into its third year in 1863, the main focus of the fighting remained in the East. There the forces and fortunes of the two sides—North and South—were about to converge in the conflict's great turning point.

CHAPTER 4
AFRICAN-AMERICAN SOLDIERS

The idea of blacks' fighting in the Union Army was at first very controversial. The famous northern black orator and abolitionist Frederick Douglass held that allowing blacks to fight would be a boon for the Union. Also, he argued, blacks who fought for their country would be widely seen as earning their citizenship. "Once let the black man get upon his person the brass letters U.S.," he said, "let him get [a] musket on his shoulder and bullets in his pocket, and there is no power on earth which can deny that he has earned the right to citizenship in the United States."

But white leaders, in the North as well as the South, initially refused to allow blacks to fight. In the North, some free African-American men tried to enlist when the war started. But they were turned away. A law enacted in 1792 prohibited blacks from serving in the country's armed forces. But a more pressing reason for excluding blacks existed in the corridors of power. Lincoln and his advisers feared that enlisting them would incite some loyal slave states, including Maryland, to secede.

★SWEEPING NEW LEGISLATION

This situation changed in short order, however. After First Bull Run and other early battles, it became clear that the war would be long and large-scale. Northern leaders realized they needed all the able-bodied soldiers they could find. In July 1862 Congress passed the Militia Act. It stated that the president was "authorized to receive into the service of the United States, for the purpose of … any military or naval service for which they may be found competent, persons of African descent, and such persons shall be enrolled and organized under such regulations … as the President may prescribe."

The act also said: "Persons of African descent, who under this law shall be employed, shall receive ten dollars

A young African-American served as a drummer boy during the Civil War.

per month and one ration, three dollars of which monthly pay may be in clothing." (In contrast, white soldiers then received $13 per month with no deductions for their clothing. Though blacks were now allowed to serve, they were clearly not treated as equals.)

Other new and sweeping legislation followed. On July 19, slavery was abolished in all U.S. territories. And a few days later, Lincoln told his Cabinet that he had decided to issue an Emancipation Proclamation. He issued it in September 1862, and it officially went into effect January 1, 1863. The proclamation stated that all black slaves in the Confederacy were now and in the future free.

The document had two main limitations, though.

A PLEA FOR EQUAL PAY

For African-Americans, one glaring drawback of the 1862 Militia Act was that it provided lower pay for black soldiers than for white ones. In 1863 James H. Gooding, a freeborn black in the 54th Massachusetts Infantry, wrote to President Lincoln, saying in part:

"We are fully armed and equipped, have done all the various Duties, pertaining to a Soldiers life. [And] when the war trumpet sounded o'er the land ... the Black man laid his life at the Altar of the Nation. ... We have done a Soldiers Duty. Why cant we have a Soldiers pay? ... We appeal to You, Sir: as the Executive of the Nation, to have us Justly Dealt with."

Lincoln announced the Emancipation Proclamation September 22, 1862.

First, it was mostly symbolic. The fact that the U.S. government had declared southern slaves free meant nothing to Confederates—only military victories would make the proclamation effective. Slaves behind Confederate lines remained in servitude. Second, ending slavery was a secondary goal to Lincoln in issuing the proclamation. His main purpose was to restore the Union. If southern slaves resisted their masters or ran away, so much the better, because it would weaken the Confederacy. He also hoped it would strike a blow to the South's economy and military. On August 22, 1862, the president explained his thinking on the matter:

"My paramount object in this struggle *is* to save the Union, and is *not* either to save or to destroy slavery. If I could save the Union without freeing *any* slave I would do it, and if I could save it by freeing *all* the slaves I would do it; and if I could save it by freeing some and leaving others alone I would also do that. What I do about slavery, and the colored race, I do because I believe it helps to save the Union."

★"PRISON DOOR" OPENS

Confederate reactions to the Emancipation Proclamation were predictable. Most southern whites denounced it—and Lincoln—and vowed to keep slavery alive.
In the North, reaction was mixed. Some northerners complained bitterly that the focus of the war had changed from saving the Union to ending slavery. Others celebrated when the document took effect in January 1863. Abolitionists, who had fought long and

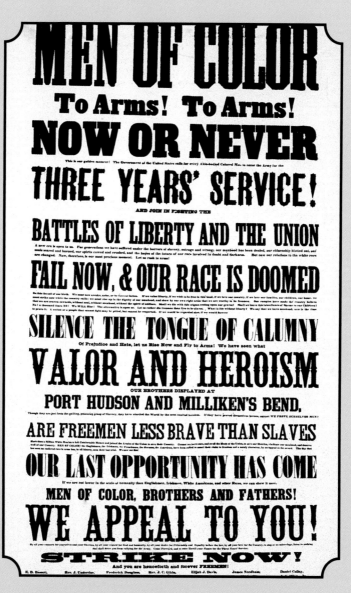

A recruitment poster signed by Frederick Douglass and others encouraged blacks to fight for the Union.

hard to end slavery, were especially thrilled. "The iron gate of our prison stands half open," Frederick Douglass said in a speech urging blacks to enlist in the Army.

"One gallant rush from the North will fling it wide open, while four millions of our brothers and sisters shall march out into liberty. The chance is now given you to end in a day the bondage of centuries, and to rise in one bound [step] from social degradation to the plane of common equality with all other varieties of men."

A celebration of a different sort took place on the Union-held Sea Islands, off South Carolina's coast. There, another abolitionist, Colonel Thomas W. Higginson, had for several months been in charge of a special project. He had organized and was still training

JUST AS EFFECTIVE AS WHITES

While training black soldiers, Union officer Thomas W. Higginson learned that they were every bit as competent and effective as white soldiers. He later wrote:

"It needs but a few days to show the absurdity of distrusting the military [abilities] of these people. They have quite as much average comprehension as whites … as much courage … as much previous knowledge of the gun, and, above all, a readiness of ear. … There is no trouble about the drill; they will surpass whites in that."

the first Union regiment entirely made up of former black slaves—the 1st South Carolina Volunteers.

When news arrived that Lincoln had signed the Emancipation Proclamation, freeing all the blacks in the Confederacy, the members of the regiment, along with many whites, gathered before an American flag. There the document was read aloud.

Then, Higginson later wrote, "followed an incident so simple, so touching, so utterly unexpected and startling, that I can scarcely believe it on recalling, though it gave the key-note to the whole day. The very moment the speaker had ceased, and just as I took and waved the flag, which now for the first time meant anything to these poor people, there suddenly arose [three black voices singing] 'My Country, 'tis of thee, Sweet land of liberty, Of thee I sing!' … Firmly and irrepressibly the quavering voices sang on, verse after verse; others of the colored people joined in … I never saw anything so electric; it made all other words cheap; it seemed the choked voice of a race at last unloosed."

As news of the proclamation spread through the South, some slaves escaped their masters and sought protection in the North. Both they and many already free northern blacks helped in the war effort in noncombat roles. Some worked on military construction projects. Others willingly labored for southern businessmen who had remained loyal to the Union. Still others leased land from the government and hired other freed blacks to work for them. The former slaves learned to become self-sufficient.

★THE LEGENDARY 54TH

As the months rolled by, more and more African-American men began serving as full-fledged soldiers in all-black units led by white officers. The most famous was the 54th Massachusetts Volunteer Infantry Regiment. The state's governor, John A. Andrew, organized it early in 1863. Under their white commander, Colonel Robert Gould Shaw, members of the 54th first faced the horrors of battle on July 16 of that year. They successfully pushed back a Confederate attack on James Island, in South Carolina.

Two days later, the unit was ordered to assault Fort Wagner, a well-fortified Confederate stronghold in Charleston harbor. Witnesses claimed that Shaw's men performed with the utmost professionalism and courage. More than 100 of them, including Shaw, died in the attack. And though they were unable to capture the fort, their heroic effort (accurately depicted in the 1989 film *Glory*) became legendary.

The charge at Fort Wagner inspired other African-Americans to serve. By the end of the war, the Union Army had 179,000 blacks, about 10 percent of its total.

The bravery shown by the 54th Regiment boosted recruitment in the Union Army.

Another 19,000 blacks served in the Navy. President Lincoln later credited the service of African-American soldiers and sailors as a significant factor in the Union's ultimate victory. In this way, Frederick Douglass' prediction was fulfilled. Many former slaves proved they could fight for their country—even to their deaths—as well as any white citizens could.

CHAPTER 5

A GREAT TURNING POINT

In a way, the Union loss at Chancellorsville in early May 1863 led to the war's most famous battle and greatest single turning point. President Lincoln and his commander at Chancellorsville, Major General Joseph Hooker, had hoped to deliver a decisive defeat to Robert E. Lee's army in that battle. That would have opened the way for Union forces to capture Richmond at last.

Their hopes had been dashed, however. Though badly outnumbered, Lee had soundly defeated Hooker. Southern leaders, including Lee, were emboldened by the victory and saw it as an opportunity to launch a second invasion of northern territory. To that end, Lee led his army into southern Pennsylvania later in May. He hoped to seize Harrisburg, and, if possible, even Philadelphia or Washington, D.C. Such gains, he thought, might persuade the North to stop fighting. Lincoln was mightily disappointed in Hooker's performance during the Union defeat at Chancellorsville, and

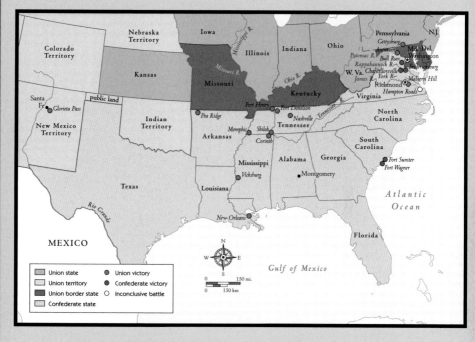

The Battle of Gettysburg was the only major Civil War battle fought in the North.

he replaced him with Major General George G. Meade. To counter Lee's offensive, Meade moved a large force of troops through southern Pennsylvania. Near the small town of Gettysburg, the two armies would meet and change the course of history. About that fateful encounter, the historian Henry S. Commager wrote:

"It was the greatest single battle ever fought in North America [and] marked by some of the heaviest fighting in the war. ... No other single battle combined so dramatically so many memorable scenes and events."

★THE FIRST DAY

Lee and Meade seem to have had the same early strategy. Each looked for a strong position to occupy and planned to wait there for the enemy to attack. As so often happens with initial military preparations, however, things did not go as planned. On July 1 a group of Confederate soldiers headed to Gettysburg hoping to find shoes, which for them were in short supply. Northwest of town, they unexpectedly encountered a group of Union horsemen. The two units began fighting.

What started as a mere skirmish soon grew into a battle of epic proportions. As news of the fighting spread, units from both armies hurried to the scene. When Lee arrived, he told two of his officers to attack the forming Union line. In a series of charges, Confederate units assaulted the northern troops, who managed to hold on until midafternoon. Eventually, however, they were overwhelmed. One of the Union generals, Oliver O. Howard, ordered a retreat to Cemetery Ridge, not far south of the town.

Lee realized that Cemetery Ridge was the proverbial "high ground," from which an army could command the entire area. He was determined to seize it. But he knew it would not be easy, since it was well fortified with enemy cannons and infantry. Lee ordered one of his officers, Richard S. Ewell, to take the hill. But Ewell, who was

The Battle of Gettysburg lasted three days, and thousands of soldiers were killed.

worried about the difficulties involved, hesitated and never attacked that day. This turned out to be one of the major lost opportunities of both the battle and the war. During the hours in which Ewell held back, Meade shrewdly sent in more of his own men. They strengthened the Union line, which by nightfall extended for more than two miles (three kilometers).

★THE SECOND DAY

On the second day of fighting, July 2, Lee's strategy remained the same. He was unwavering in his desire to capture the high ground. By now, that included not only Cemetery Ridge, but also other nearby hills that Meade's men had fortified.

Lee discussed his plan with General James Longstreet, his second-in-command. Longstreet advised Lee not to pursue the assault. The Union position on the hills was simply too strong, Longstreet argued. But Lee was

A Confederate charge was painted by A.C. Redwood, who was in the Battle of Gettysburg.

inflexible. "The enemy is there," he said, "and I am going to strike him!" Even though Longstreet lost the argument, he did as Lee ordered and attacked. Confederate forces under Longstreet and other officers threw themselves headlong at Union positions on and around a hill called Little Round Top. But Meade and his officers benefited from well-constructed defenses and the arrival of more reinforcements. When the sun set on day two, the Union positions on the hills were still intact.

★"HOPELESS SLAUGHTER"

On the third day, Lee once more set his sights on breaking the enemy lines on the hills. He met again with Longstreet and told him to attack the Union center, on Cemetery Ridge. The main tool of the assault, Lee said, would be a force of about 14,000 soldiers led by George E. Pickett and two other Confederate officers.

Longstreet again argued against a frontal attack on such a well-entrenched enemy. But Lee refused to budge and gave the final order. Longstreet later recalled: "My heart was heavy. I could see the desperate and hopeless nature of the charge and the hopeless slaughter it would cause."

History proved Longstreet right. "Pickett's Charge," as posterity came to call it, was both monumental in scope and filled with heroic acts. It was also horrifyingly bloody and failed to achieve its goal. More than half of those who took part in the fatal charge were killed, wounded, or captured. Confederate officer Charles S. Peyton, who commanded one of the brigades in Pickett's unit, later wrote a detailed report of the charge that had approached the Union lines posted behind a stone wall. It said in part:

"Our line, much shattered, still kept up the advance until within about 20 paces of the wall, when, for a moment, it recoiled under the terrific fire that poured into our ranks both from their batteries and from their sheltered infantry. [We] rushed forward with unyielding determination. [And] … the fighting over the wall became hand to hand, and of the most desperate character; but more than half having already fallen, our line was found too weak to rout the enemy. [We became] greatly scattered, the identity of every regiment being entirely lost, and every regimental commander killed or wounded."

George E. Pickett (right) received orders for the fatal assault that would bear his name.

The chaos and deafening roar during the enormous charges at Gettysburg were ably captured by a Confederate soldier named John Dooley:

"The earth mountains and sky seem to open and darken the air with smoke and death dealing missiles. Never will I forget those scenes and sounds. The earth seems unsteady beneath this furious cannonading, and the air might be said to be agitated by the wings of death. Over 400 guns [cannons] nearly every minute being discharged!"

An English observer, Arthur Fremantle, watched as the bedraggled survivors, some of them badly wounded, retreated under fire:

"Many of them asked in piteous tones the way to the doctor or an ambulance. The farther I got, the greater became the number of the wounded. … Some were walking alone on crutches composed of two rifles, others supported by men less badly wounded than themselves. … They were still under a heavy fire; the shells were continually … carrying further destruction amongst this melancholy procession."

★FORCED ONTO THE DEFENSIVE

About 164,000 solders took part in the mighty three-day struggle at Gettysburg, and both sides suffered terribly. About 28,000 Confederates and roughly 23,000 Union soldiers were killed, wounded, or missing.

But it was not the large casualty figures alone that made Gettysburg a turning point. Lee was forced to retreat into Confederate territory. Never again was the South able to mount a major offensive against the North.

Almost two more years of grueling, often lethal fighting

A photograph taken July 4, 1863, of the dead at Gettysburg was titled A Harvest of Death.

still lay ahead for the opposing sides. Throughout the rest of the war, the Confederacy would be on the defensive as Union armies forced it into a death struggle for its very existence. Many in the South already guessed the final outcome. "Yesterday we rode on the pinnacle of success," a Confederate officer wrote about three weeks after Gettysburg. "Today, absolute ruin seems to be our portion. The Confederacy totters [stumbles] to its destruction."

THE GETTYSBURG ADDRESS

In November 1863 the government made the Gettysburg battlefield a permanent cemetery for those who had died there. At the ceremony, on November 19, a famous orator named Edward Everett was the main speaker. History has forgotten his words, though, because President Lincoln was there too. The mere 10 sentences he spoke—the Gettysburg Address—later came to be seen as one of the finest and most moving speeches of all time. It ends with the words:

"We here highly resolve that these dead shall not have died in vain, that this nation under God shall have a new birth of freedom, and that government of the people, by the people, for the people shall not perish from the earth."

TIMELINE

1860

November: Abraham Lincoln is elected president of the United States

December: South Carolina secedes from the Union

1861

February: Seven seceded states form the Confederate States of America

March: Lincoln is inaugurated

April: Confederate forces attack and capture Fort Sumter, in South Carolina

July: The South wins the war's first major battle at Bull Run, in Virginia

1862

1863

February: Northern forces capture Tennessee's capital, Nashville

March: The Union wins a major victory at Pea Ridge, in Arkansas; armies clash at Glorieta Pass, in New Mexico Territory

April: Northern soldiers under General Ulysses S. Grant take Forts Henry and Donelson, and win a slim victory at Shiloh, in Tennessee

July: Congress passes the Militia Act, calling for recruiting African-American soldiers; Union forces win at Malvern Hill, in Virginia, one of their only victories in the Peninsula Campaign

August: A Confederate army wins a second fight at Bull Run

September: One of the war's bloodiest battles takes place at Antietam Creek, in Maryland

December: Union forces suffer heavy losses at Fredericksburg, in Virginia

January: President Lincoln's Emancipation Proclamation, freeing slaves in the South, becomes official

May: The South wins a major victory at Chancellorsville, in north-central Virginia

July: Union forces win a huge battle at Gettysburg, in Pennsylvania; African-American soldiers fighting for the Union assault Fort Wagner, in South Carolina, gaining lasting fame

November: Lincoln delivers his famous Gettysburg Address

GLOSSARY

abolitionist: person who supported the banning of slavery

artillery: large guns, such as cannons

battery: group or unit of cannons and the men operating them

bayonet: sharp blade attached to the end of a musket or rifle; it is used as a weapon in close combat

bedraggled: messed up or untidy

bow: front of a ship

brigade: military group of fighting units consisting of several regiments

canister: cylindrical container filled with small musketballs or other metal objects and fired by a cannon

Confederacy: southern states that fought against the northern states in the Civil War; also called the Confederate States of America

federal: national, or having to do with the U.S. government

fortitude: strength of mind that enables one to endure pain or adversity with courage

gunboat: small ship outfitted with cannons and other guns

inauguration: formal ceremony to swear a person into political office

infantry: soldiers who fight on foot

musket: early gun that fired when a flame ignited gunpowder in a small pan

plantation: large farm in the South, usually worked by slaves

posterity: all future generations

proclamation: official announcement

regiment: large infantry unit; in the Civil War, it had about 1,000 men

secede: withdraw from a nation or group

servitude: slavery

shell: metal container filled with gunpowder and fired from a cannon

Union: the northern and loyal border states that fought against the southern states in the Civil War

Yankee: nickname for a northerner; Union army soldier during the Civil War

ADDITIONAL RESOURCES

FURTHER READING

Brownell, Richard. *The Civil War: The Fall of the Confederacy and the End of Slavery.* San Diego: Thomson/Gale, 2005.

Haugen, Brenda. *Ulysses S. Grant: Union General and U.S. President.* Minneapolis: Compass Point Books, 2005.

Johnson, Jennifer. *Gettysburg: The Bloodiest Battle of the Civil War.* New York: Franklin Watts, 2010.

Murphy, Jim. *A Savage Thunder: Antietam and the Bloody Road to Freedom.* New York: Margaret K. McElderry Books, 2009.

Nardo, Don. *Mathew Brady: The Camera Is the Eye of History.* Berkeley Heights, N.J.: Enslow, 2009.

Reis, Ronald A. *African Americans and the Civil War.* New York: Chelsea House Publishers, 2009.

INTERNET SITES

FactHound offers a safe, fun way to find Internet sites related to this book. All of the sites on FactHound have been researched by our staff.

Here's all you do:

Visit *www.facthound.com*

Type in this code: 9780756543686

Read all the books in the Civil War series:

A Nation Divided: The Long Road to the Civil War

Bull Run to Gettysburg: Early Battles of the Civil War

North Over South: Final Victory in the Civil War

Reconstruction: Rebuilding America after the Civil War

SELECT BIBLIOGRAPHY

Anderson, Bern. *By Sea and River: The Naval History of the Civil War.* New York: Da Capo Press, 1989.

Axelrod, Alan. *The War Between the Spies: A History of Espionage During the American Civil War.* New York: Atlantic Monthly Press, 1992.

Bearss, Edwin C. *Fields of Honor.* Washington, D.C.: National Geographic Society, 2006.

Buell, Thomas B. *The Warrior Generals: Combat Leadership in the Civil War.* New York: Crown Publishers, 1997.

Catton, Bruce. *American Heritage New History of the Civil War.* New York: Viking, 1996.

Catton, Bruce. *Gettysburg: The Final Fury.* Garden City, N.Y.: Doubleday, 1974.

Catton, Bruce. *Glory Road: The Bloody Route From Fredericksburg to Gettysburg.* Garden City, N.Y.: Doubleday, 1952.

Catton, Bruce. *Mr. Lincoln's Army.* Garden City, N.Y.: Doubleday, 1951.

Catton, Bruce. *A Stillness at Appomattox.* Garden City, N.Y.: Doubleday, 1953.

Coggins, Jack. *Arms and Equipment of the Civil War.* Mineola, N.Y.: Dover Publications, 2004.

Commager, Henry S., ed. *The Blue and the Gray: The Story of the Civil War as Told by Its Participants.* New York: Bobbs-Merrill, 1991.

Drury, Ian, and Tony Gibbons. *The Civil War Military Machine: Weapons and Tactics of the Union and Confederate Armed Forces.* New York: Smithmark, 1993.

Eicher, David J. *The Longest Night: A Military History of the Civil War.* New York: Simon and Schuster, 2001.

Foote, Shelby. *Stars in Their Courses: The Gettysburg Campaign, June–July 1863.* New York: Modern Library, 1994.

Griffith, Paddy. *Battle Tactics of the Civil War.* New Haven: Yale University Press, 2001.

Hansen, Harry. *The Civil War: A History.* New York: New American Library, 2001.

Hyslop, Stephen G. *Eyewitness to the Civil War: The Complete History From Secession to Reconstruction.* Washington, D.C.: National Geographic, 2006.

Jones, Archer. *Civil War Command and Strategy: The Process of Victory and Defeat.* New York: Free Press, 1992.

Marten, James. *Civil War America: Voices From the Home Front.* Santa Barbara, Calif.: ABC-CLIO, 2003.

McPherson, James M. *Battle Cry of Freedom: The Civil War Era.* New York: Oxford University Press, 2003.

Morison, Samuel E. *The Oxford History of the American People.* New York: Oxford University Press, 1965.

Oates, Stephen B. *The Whirlwind of War: Voices of the Storm, 1861–1865.* New York: Harper Collins, 1998.

Post, Lydia M., ed. *Soldiers' Letters from Camp, Battlefield, and Prison.* New York: Bunce and Huntington, 1865.

Zeller, Bob. *The Blue and Gray in Black and White: A History of Civil War Photography.* Westport, Conn.: Praeger, 2005.

SOURCE NOTES

Editor's note: For the most part, three main sources were used when quoting casualty figures:

David J. Eicher. *The Longest Night: A Military History of the Civil War*. New York: Simon and Schuster, 2001.

Stephen G. Hyslop. *Eyewitness to the Civil War: The Complete History From Secession to Reconstruction*. Washington, D.C.: National Geographic, 2006.

James McPherson. *Battle Cry of Freedom: The Civil War Era*. New York: Oxford University Press, 2003.

Page 7, line 4: Henry S. Commager, ed. *The Blue and the Gray: The Story of the Civil War as Told by Its Participants*. New York: Bobbs-Merrill, 1991, p. 66.

Page 7, line 14: Allan Nevins. *The War for the Union, Vol. 1*. New York: Scribner, 1959, p. 75.

Page 7, line 16: Grady McWhiney and Perry D. Jamieson. *Attack and Die: Civil War Military Tactics and the Southern Heritage*. Tuscaloosa: University of Alabama Press, 1984, p. 170.

Page 8, line 3: Eric Foner and John A. Garraty, eds. *The Reader's Companion to American History*. Boston: Houghton Mifflin, 1991, p. 186.

Page 9, line 7: Samuel E. Morison. *The Oxford History of the American People*. New York: Oxford University Press, 1965, pp. 615–616.

Page 10, sidebar, line 6: Thomas Cooper DeLeon. *Four Years in Rebel Capitals: An Inside View of Life in the Southern Confederacy, From Birth to Death*. Whitefish, Mont.: Kessinger Publishing, 2006, p. 91.

Page 11, line 10: Frederick Maurice, ed. *An Aide-de-Camp of Lee, Papers of Colonel Charles Marshall*. Boston: Little, Brown, and Company, 1927, pp. 17–18.

Page 14, line 8: Lydia M. Post, ed. *Soldiers' Letters from Camp, Battlefield, and Prison*. New York: Bunce and Huntington, 1865, p. 112.

Page 16, line 14: Frank Moore, ed. *The Rebellion Record: A Diary of American Events, Vol. 2*. New York: G.P. Putnam, 1861, pp. 93–94.

Page 18, line 2: Paddy Griffith. *Battle Tactics of the Civil War*. New Haven: Yale University Press, 2001, p. 30.

Page 20, sidebar, line 5: Oliver W. Norton. *Army Letters, 1861–1865*. Chicago: O.L. Deming, 1903, p. 92.

Page 21, line 20: *The Blue and the Gray: The Story of the Civil War as Told by Its Participants*, p. 129.

Page 22, sidebar, line 6: Ibid., pp. 135–136.

Page 23, line 22: Rufus R. Dawes. *Service with the Sixth Wisconsin Volunteers*. Marietta, Ohio: E.R. Alderman and Sons, 1890, p. 90.

Page 25, line 11: James Dunn. "The Angel of the Battlefield." Undated newspaper clipping in Clara Barton Papers, Library of Congress.

Page 26, line 20: Mr. Lincoln's White House: Noah Brooks (1830–1903). 11 March 2010. www.mrlincolnswhitehouse.org/inside.asp?ID=41&subjectID=2

Page 29, line 6: William Watson. *Life in the Confederate Army*. New York: Scribner and Welford, 1888, p. 320.

Page 30, sidebar, line 5: Leander Stillwell. *The Story of a Common Soldier of Army Life in the Civil War, 1861–1865*. Kansas City: Franklin Hudson Publishing Company, 1920, p. 44.

Page 31, line 6: *The Blue and the Gray: The Story of the Civil War as Told by Its Participants*, p. 807.

Page 32, line 4: Susan Perkins, ed. *Letters of Capt. George Hamilton Perkins*. Concord, N.H.: I.C. Evans, 1886, pp. 69–70.

Page 33, line 5: Kate M. Rowland and Mrs. Morris L. Croxall, eds. *The Journal of Julia LeGrand, New Orleans, 1862–1863*. Richmond, Va.: Everett Waddy, 1911, pp. 39–43.

Page 34, line 10: *Official Reports of Battles, as Published by Order of the Confederate Congress at Richmond*. New York: Charles B. Richardson, 1863, pp. 187–188.

Page 35, sidebar, line 4: Ibid., pp. 188–189.

Page 36, line 6: *Eyewitness to the Civil War: The Complete History From Secession to Reconstruction*, p. 253.

Page 37, line 7: "The Militia Act, July 17, 1862." Freedmen & Southern Society Project. 11 March 2010. www.history.umd.edu/ Freedmen/milact.htm

Page 38, sidebar, line 6: "Letter from Corporal James Henry Gooding to President Lincoln, September 28, 1863." Primary Sources: Workshops in American History. 11 March 2010. www.learner.org/workshops/primarysources/ emancipation/docs/jhgooding.html

Page 40, line 8: "Abraham Lincoln's Letter to Horace Greeley." Abraham Lincoln Online. 11 March 2010. http://showcase.netins.net/ web/creative/lincoln/speeches/greeley.htm

Page 41, line 1: "Frederick Douglass: Men of Color, To Arms!" BlackPast.org. 11 March 2010. www.blackpast.org/?q=1863-frederick-douglass-men-color-arms

Page 42, sidebar, line 4: Thomas W. Higginson. *Army Life in a Black Regiment*. Boston: Lee and Shepard, 1890, p. 134.

Page 43, line 8: Ibid., p. 139.

Page 44, line 23: "Black Soldiers in the Civil War." The National Archives. 11 March 2010. www.archives.gov/education/lessons/ blacks-civil-war/

Page 47, line 7: *The Blue and the Gray: The Story of the Civil War as Told by Its Participants*, pp. 589–590.

Page 51, line 1: Shelby Foote. *Stars in Their Courses: The Gettysburg Campaign, June–July 1863*. New York: Modern Library, 1994, p. 175.

Page 51, line 19: Clarence C. Buel and Robert U. Johnson, *Battles and Leaders of the Civil War*, Vol. 3. New York: The Century Company, 1888, p. 345.

Page 52, line 7: "Confederate Report on Pickett's Charge." The American Civil War: The Battle of Gettysburg. 11 March 2010. www.brotherswar.com/Gettysburg-3r.htm

Page 53, sidebar, line 4: America Past and Present Online: John Dooley, Passages from a Journal (1863). 11 March 2010. http://wps.ablongman. com/wps/media/objects/245/251530/primary sources1_15_1.html

Page 53, line 4: The Longstreet Chronicles. 11 March 2010. www.longstreetchronicles. org/getty3.htm

Page 55, line 5: Frank E. Vandiver, ed. *The Civil War Diary of General Josiah Gorgas*. Tuscaloosa: University of Alabama Press, 1947, p. 55.

Page 55, sidebar, line 10: "The Gettysburg Address." The Avalon Project: Documents in Law, History and Diplomacy. 11 March 2010. http://avalon.law.yale.edu/19th_ century/gettyb.asp

INDEX

African-American soldiers, 36, 37–38, 42–43, 44–45

Barton, Clara, 25
Battle of Antietam, 23–25
Battle of Bull Run (First), 15–16, 16–18, 19, 37
Battle of Bull Run (Second), 23
Battle of Chancellorsville, 26, 46
Battle of Fredericksburg, 25–26
Battle of Gaines' Mill, 20
Battle of Gettysburg, 47, 48–49, 50–51, 51–53, 54, 55
Battle of Glorieta Pass, 34–35
Battle of James Island, 44
Battle of Malvern Hill, 21
Battle of Nashville, 27–28
Battle of New Orleans, 31–33
Battle of Pea Ridge, 28–29
Battle of Shiloh, 30, 31
Beauregard, P.G.T., 15–16, 30

Burnside, Ambrose, 25–26

Confederate States of America, 5, 15
Confederate Territory of Arizona, 33–35

Davis, Jefferson, 5, 7, 22
Douglass, Frederick, 36, 41–42, 45

Eastern Theater, 15
Emancipation Proclamation, 38–40, 40–42, 43
Ewell, Richard S., 48–49

forts, 6, 8, 29, 31, 44

Gettysburg Address, 55
Grant, Ulysses S., 29, 30

Higginson, Thomas W., 42–43
Hooker, Joseph, 26, 46–47

ironclads, 12–14

Jackson, Thomas "Stonewall," 23, 26

Lee, Robert E., 21–22, 23, 24, 25, 26, 46, 47, 48, 50–51, 54
Lincoln, Abraham, 4, 5, 6, 15, 19, 26, 31, 33, 36, 38, 39–40, 43, 45, 46–47, 55
Longstreet, James, 23, 50–51

maps, 9, 47
McClellan, George B., 19–20, 21
McDowell, Irvin, 16, 19
Meade, George G., 47, 48, 49, 50, 51
Militia Act (1862), 37–38

Peninsula Campaign, 19–22
"Pickett's Charge," 51–53

railroads, 11, 28, 29, 30

Sea Islands, 42–43
secession, 4, 5, 6, 36
slavery, 4–5, 36, 38–40, 40–41, 42–44, 45

weapons, 10–11, 12, 27–28
Western Theater, 27, 33

ABOUT THE AUTHOR

Historian and award-winning author Don Nardo has written many books for young people about American history. He lives with his wife, Christine, in Massachusetts.